PLAYING
PRO
SPORTS

★ PLAYING PRO ★
BASEBALL

Brian Howell

Lerner Publications Company ● Minneapolis

Lerner Publications Company
A division of Lerner Publishing Group, Inc.
241 First Avenue North
Minneapolis, MN 55401 USA

For reading levels and more information, look up this title at
www.lernerbooks.com.

Content Consultant: Gabe Kapler, 12-year MLB veteran

Library of Congress Cataloging-in-Publication Data

Howell, Brian, 1974–
    Playing pro baseball / by Brian Howell.
      pages   cm. — (Playing pro sports)
    Includes index.
    ISBN 978–1–4677–3846–0 (lib. bdg. : alk. paper)
    ISBN 978–1–4677–4726–4 (eBook)
    1. Baseball—Juvenile literature. 2. Professional sports—Juvenile literature. I. Title.
  GV867.5.H69 2015
  796.357—dc23   2013048604

Manufactured in the United States of America
1 – PC – 7/15/14

CONTENTS

CHAPTER ONE

PLAY BALL!

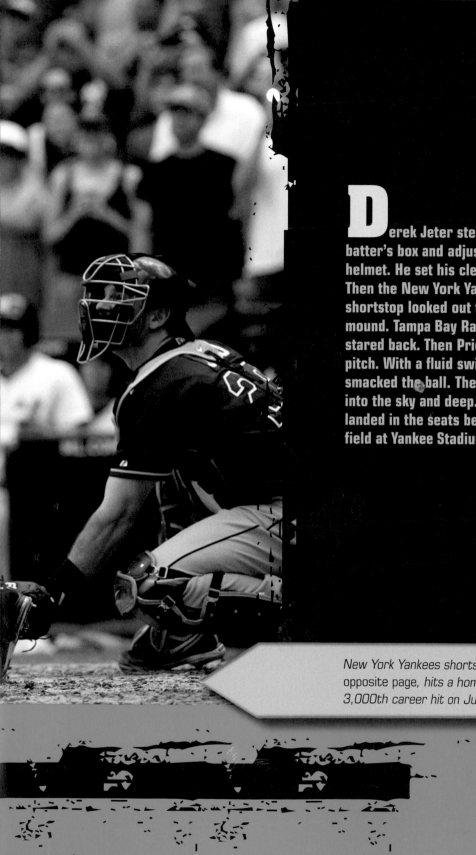

Derek Jeter stepped into the batter's box and adjusted his batting helmet. He set his cleats in the dirt. Then the New York Yankees' star shortstop looked out to the pitcher's mound. Tampa Bay Rays ace David Price stared back. Then Price delivered the pitch. With a fluid swing, Jeter's bat smacked the ball. The ball sailed high into the sky and deep. Finally, the ball landed in the seats beyond left-center field at Yankee Stadium.

New York Yankees shortstop Derek Jeter, opposite page, *hits a home run for his 3,000th career hit on July 9, 2011.*

Jeter quickly circled the bases after the home run. Upon his arrival at home plate, his teammates took turns hugging him and congratulating him. Many of the 48,103 fans in the Yankee Stadium stands chanted, "Der-ek Je-ter! Der-ek Je-ter!"

That home run came on July 9, 2011. It was Jeter's 3,000th career hit. The 3,000-hit mark is one of the great milestones in baseball. Through the 2013 season, Jeter was one of just 28 players in baseball history who had done it.

To achieve 3,000 hits is the sign of a special career. Many talented hitters have come and gone over the years. Only the very best hitters can produce long enough to reach 3,000 hits. That means they must stay in good shape and avoid injuries. It also means continuing to find new ways to perform at the top level. Jeter exemplified all of those things throughout his career with the Yankees.

Quotable

"We learned at a very, very young age that there are expectations. You want to get good grades, be involved in a lot of things in school. You may not appreciate it, but as you get older, they really set the tone for setting goals and working real hard to achieve them.

"When my career is said and done, I don't want to look back and say, 'Well, I wish I would have worked harder.' Don't let anyone tell you that your goals are too high and unreachable, because if you work hard, you can attain them."

—New York Yankees shortstop Derek Jeter

Derek Jeter waves to the crowd at Yankee Stadium after he recorded his 3,000th hit on July 9, 2011.

America's Pastime

Baseball is known as America's pastime. That is because the sport has been around since the early 1800s. Other popular sports such as basketball, football, hockey, and soccer were not invented until later. All of those sports are popular today. During the late 1800s and the early 1900s, however, baseball was by far the most popular team sport in the United States.

Baseball's popularity began to take off soon after the Civil War (1861–1865). More and more people began playing the game. That led to more organization and greater competitiveness on the amateur level. Then, in 1869, the Cincinnati Red Stockings began seeking out the best players and paying them salaries. That made the Red Stockings the first professional baseball team.

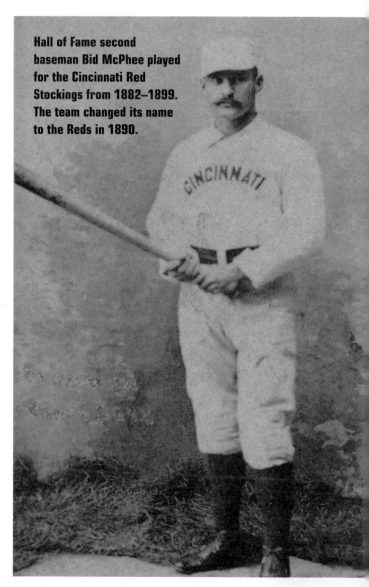

Hall of Fame second baseman Bid McPhee played for the Cincinnati Red Stockings from 1882–1899. The team changed its name to the Reds in 1890.

Seven years later, in 1876, the National League (NL) formed. The American League (AL) followed in 1901. Both leagues had eight teams in 1901. Those leagues make up Major League Baseball (MLB). And since 1903, the AL and NL champions have played each other in the World Series.

Baseball has grown over the years. The AL and NL each have 15 teams. Those teams play in large, fancy ballparks. The minimum salary for players in 2013 was $490,000. Twenty-one players earned more than $20 million that season. The basics of the game are the same as ever, though. Hitting a pitch in 2014 is pretty much the same as hitting a pitch in 1901. Players have more sophisticated training plans than in the past. Yet player output has remained mostly consistent. Fans can compare the output of modern sluggers such as Albert Pujols with legendary players such as

Media Stars

Fans are not allowed into baseball clubhouses. They must rely on reporters to provide inside information about the teams and players. Dealing with the press is a daily occurrence for MLB players. Reporters are around throughout spring training. During the season, they are allowed into the clubhouse for a period before and after every game. Reporters ask the players questions about everything from that day's game to injuries to the players' personal lives. Players have to learn how to handle the media attention. Few players have done that better than Derek Jeter. Throughout his career, he has been accommodating to the media while keeping his personal life private and avoiding negative attention.

Babe Ruth. As such, baseball's records are considered to be more sacred than the records in many other sports.

Reaching the major leagues is a major test of ability, hard work, attention to detail, and patience. Players must first learn the fundamentals of the game. Then they must perfect them to the best of their abilities. That means hours upon hours practicing baseball skills. It means studying the game to understand its nuances. It also means staying in peak physical condition for MLB's long 162-game season. The smallest detail in baseball could mean the difference between being a minor-league lifer and a major-league star.

IN THE SPOTLIGHT

Troy Tulowitzki dazzled fans as a rookie for the Colorado Rockies in 2007. He proved to be a great hitter and also a top defensive shortstop. Tulowitzki led NL shortstops in fielding percentage (.987), putouts (262), assists (561), and double plays (114). He also turned the 13th unassisted triple play in major-league history.

Tulowitzki is known for his aggressive approach and powerful throwing arm. He said he always tries to throw with a four-seam grip. That is a grip in which the index and middle fingers are placed across the baseball's perpendicular seam. The thumb is on the bottom of the baseball.

"What a four-seam grip will help you do is throw the ball as straight as you possibly can so we can cut down on our throwing errors," he said. "Then, I'm not afraid to mess around in practice, throwing from different arm angles."

CHAPTER TWO

GETTING THERE

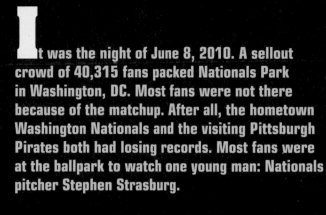

It was the night of June 8, 2010. A sellout crowd of 40,315 fans packed Nationals Park in Washington, DC. Most fans were not there because of the matchup. After all, the hometown Washington Nationals and the visiting Pittsburgh Pirates both had losing records. Most fans were at the ballpark to watch one young man: Nationals pitcher Stephen Strasburg.

Fans had known of the talented 21-year-old right-hander for years. He had dominated in college and the minor leagues. On this night, Strasburg finally made his major-league debut. It was one of the most anticipated nights in team history.

Washington Nationals pitcher Stephen Strasburg pitches during his major-league debut on June 8, 2010.

Strasburg was one of baseball's most famous prospects. But like almost all MLB players, he first had to prove himself in the minor leagues. Each MLB team has at least six farm teams. Those teams are split among five minor-league levels. It is extremely rare for players to skip the minor leagues. Strasburg was 21 when he took the

Stephen Strasburg pitches for the Syracuse Chiefs in May 2010. The Chiefs are the Triple-A affiliate of the Washington Nationals.

mound that night in June 2010. He played less than one season in the minors. But from 2005–2009, the average age of players making their major-league debut was 24.4. That meant most MLB players during that time had spent several years in the minors. And many more players never get out of the minor leagues.

Different Paths

Players who grow up in the United States and Canada often get their start on youth baseball fields. It is in youth baseball where players learn the basics of the game, such as proper batting and throwing techniques. These fundamentals set a foundation for future development.

As players get older, many move on to high school baseball. In many cases, players also play with a summer league squad. It is during these years that many teams begin to emphasize strategy and tactics. A strong understanding of concepts such as baserunning and positioning in the field can have a great impact on games.

How players perform at this age affects their next step.

The Draft

Every June, MLB holds a draft to select first-year players. The team with the worst record the previous season picks first. Selections go from the worst team to the best in each round. As of 2013, there were 40 rounds in the draft. Amateur players from the United States, Canada, or a US territory are eligible for the draft. After drafting a player, the team has until mid-July to try to sign that player to a contract. A player can choose not to sign and then reenter the draft the next year.

Most players stop playing organized baseball after high school. Those who are good enough sometimes go on to play in college. And some players—often those considered the best—get drafted by MLB teams and go right to the minor leagues.

MLB scouts had followed Strasburg as a high school player. However, they felt he needed to improve and get in better shape. No team selected him in the MLB draft as a high school senior. So he decided to play for the baseball team at San Diego State University. Strasburg lost weight and got stronger during his three college seasons. His raw skills also developed into dominant pitches. The Nationals then selected him first in the 2009 draft.

Joe Mauer already showed surefire skills in high school. He was a standout in three sports at Cretin-Derham Hall High School in Saint Paul, Minnesota. Mauer had an opportunity to play college football at Florida State University. But his hometown Minnesota Twins selected Mauer with the first pick in the 2001 draft. Even Mauer had to start his professional baseball career in the minor leagues, though. He debuted for the Twins in 2004. In 2009, he was named the AL Most Valuable Player (MVP).

Major-league players are increasingly coming from outside North America. Those players take different routes to reach the majors. MLB teams send scouts to watch these players in their home countries. Interested teams then offer contracts

Joe Mauer became one of baseball's most consistent hitters after the Minnesota Twins picked him first overall in the 2001 draft.

to promising teenage players. If the players get more than one offer, they can pick which team they want to sign with. From there, most players join the North American prospects in that team's farm system.

Paying Dues in the Minors

The players who reach the minor leagues are at all different skill levels. Some are top prospects like Strasburg. Washington Nationals officials knew he had the skills to pitch in the majors very soon. And Strasburg indeed debuted for the team after just 11 minor-league starts.

Most players need a lot more time to develop. Only select minor-league players are considered likely to reach the major leagues. Many players spend a few seasons in the minors before moving on to another career.

The differences between a major leaguer and a minor leaguer might look subtle. However, the details can make a huge difference in baseball. Adding a few miles per hour to a pitch makes it that much harder to hit. Improving one's bat speed or ability to recognize pitches can add several

Quotable

"I just focus on the swing and not so much the result. I just try to really work on the things I know help me: where my hand position is, how my body gets loaded, is my foot down in time. The cage is the time to think about all of those things. When you get into the game, you don't want to be thinking about that."
—Tampa Bay Rays third baseman Evan Longoria on how he practices his swing

points to a batting average. Building up strength and endurance are major focuses in the minors. Players in the minors also work to develop a better understanding of the game in areas such as baserunning and defense.

Pitcher Mark Appel works out in 2013. The Houston Astros drafted Appel first overall out of Stanford University that year and sent him to Single-A.

There is little room for error once a player reaches the major leagues. MLB players can exploit any weakness in an opposing player. So minor-league players spend countless hours working on fundamentals. These are many of the same fundamentals that the players began working on in youth baseball.

Shortstop Derek Jeter was an exceptional player in high school. The New York Yankees selected him sixth overall in the 1992 draft. Jeter still had a lot of work to do before reaching the majors, though.

IN THE SPOTLIGHT

The Kansas City Royals selected infielder Ed Lucas in the eighth round of the 2004 draft. Like most players, Lucas began his professional career in the minor leagues. Unlike most players, Lucas spent nearly a decade in the minors. Lucas reached Triple-A in 2008. That is the highest level of the minors. But Lucas spent the majority of the next five seasons there. During that time, he switched organizations twice. And at the start of the 2013 season, he joined the Miami Marlins organization and was assigned to Triple-A again.

At 31 years old, Lucas had reached an age where some thought he would never play in the majors. But finally, he made it. On May 30, 2013, Lucas made his major league debut with the Marlins. He became a regular in the lineup the rest of the season.

"I was always optimistic," Lucas said. "But in a realistic sense, I knew there was a shot I would never make it. I love the game and I want to stay in the game once I stop playing so it wasn't too big a decision for me to stick it out."

He spent four seasons in the minors before establishing himself as a major leaguer.

Jeter's need for improvement showed early. He committed 56 errors in his second minor-league season in 1993. "I knew I had to improve or I'd never make it to the Yankees—not as a shortstop anyway," Jeter wrote in his book *The Life You Imagine*.

Jeter addressed his defensive issues head-on. He spent many hours during the off-season fielding ground balls. That work paid off. Jeter not only became an all-time Yankees great—he also went on to win five Gold Glove Awards for his defense.

The hard work paid off for Strasburg too. He began playing at a young age and continued to develop as he advanced through baseball's levels. In his major-league debut in 2010, he struck out 14 Pirates while helping the Nationals get a win.

BEING AN

Once a player reaches the major leagues, he has to learn how to act and live like a major-league ballplayer. Bryce Harper had to learn those lessons much earlier than a lot of players. Harper had been a top prospect known for his power hitting. He made his major-league debut at the age of 19 on April 28, 2012. That is five years sooner than the average age of players making their MLB debuts. Harper has been a regular in the Washington Nationals' outfield ever since.

"Mentally you have to be as strong as can be," Harper said in 2012 of being in the spotlight at a young age. "I had a lot of veteran guys who really helped me out this year with that. All year long, not just on the field but off the field."

Washington Nationals outfielder Bryce Harper shows off his NL All-Star jersey before a 2012 game.

ALL-STAR

Harper quickly proved he belonged. In fact, he made the NL All-Star team in each of his first two seasons. Harper had dominated the competition throughout

Philadelphia Phillies first baseman Jim Thome stretches before a spring training game in 2012.

his youth. But thriving in the major leagues is hard even for the most skilled players. Harper played very well in May and June of his rookie year. Then he had a horrible July. He came back with a decent August, though—and he had a fantastic September. All baseball players suffer through slumps. These periods can be difficult on players. But part of being an All-Star is learning how to get out of them.

"It's just baseball," Harper said. "It's just something you have to go through and deal with. . . . Every single day, I think maybe I can go 3-for-4 tonight, or 2-for-4. You have to think the right way whether you're struggling or not."

A Long Season

Playing for an MLB team is nearly a year-round job. Each MLB team plays 162 regular-season games each year. The season usually lasts from April to September. The teams that make the playoffs play in October. The commitment goes much deeper than those six or seven months, though. Players begin reporting to spring training in February. They spend several weeks

Getaway Day

One type of day players sometimes dread is known as getaway day. This is a day when a team plays a game and immediately leaves for another city. The players have to quickly pack their belongings and head to the airport. The Minnesota Twins had one particularly difficult 13-day stretch in 2013. They played 12 games during that time. Ten of the games were on the road. The team went from Minneapolis to Detroit to Cleveland to Boston and back to Minneapolis. All teams go through similar schedules. The players must learn to live out of suitcases for half the season.

there preparing for the season and playing exhibition games.

Starting baseball activities in February means the off-season is really only three or four months long for many players. Veterans usually take a break from baseball during the off-season. They do not sit around on vacation, though. The off-season is a time for players to build strength and improve skills. This is also a time for players to undergo surgery or recover from injuries.

Not all players spend the off-season this way. Competition for spots on MLB rosters is tough. So some players play in winter leagues during the off-season. They hope to improve their skills and get noticed by scouts. There are several winter leagues. The biggest winter leagues are in Mexico, Venezuela, and the Caribbean.

Long Days

Football players have only one game per week. Basketball, hockey, and soccer players usually have two or three games per week. MLB players often play seven days per week. In fact, MLB teams can have as many as 20 consecutive days with a scheduled game.

Baseball games last approximately three hours. Game day is much longer for the players, however. They arrive at the stadium several hours before the game. A lot happens during that time.

Philadelphia Phillies pitcher Cole Hamels cools off in the dugout during a 2010 game in which the temperature reached 94°F (34°C).

Most players start the day by warming up. They might jog or ride a stationary bike to loosen up their muscles. They stretch. Some players visit the trainer. Baseball players do not have much downtime in which to recover from minor injuries. So they often play through such injuries. A trainer can treat them. Trainers also have methods to help the players be more effective while

St. Louis Cardinals players take batting and fielding practice before a 2013 playoff game at Busch Stadium in St. Louis.

injured, such as taping sprained ankles. The tape helps stabilize the ankles and prevent further injury.

Most players spend some time before games preparing for the night's opponent. Batters study opposing pitchers to gauge their tendencies. Pitchers study opposing batters to determine how best to approach them.

With so many games, baseball teams do not often have organized practices during the season. A lot of practice comes during warm-ups before games. The players take fielding practice. This is where they practice fielding, turning double plays, throwing, and other fielding skills. Each hitter also goes through batting practice. This helps him loosen up and practice hitting the ball.

For a starting pitcher, the routine is a little different. That night's starting pitcher often goes through a routine to loosen up. This usually starts with an easy game of catch. Eventually the pitcher begins long toss. Long toss is a simple game of catch in which players start near each other but eventually get as far as 300 feet (91 meters) apart. By game time, the pitcher is throwing at full speed.

Pitching is hard on the body. So pitchers are often very sore the next day. A starter throws in a game just once every five games. The day after pitching, he will do some light workouts. This gets the blood flowing and the recovery process started. Over the next three days, he will begin light throwing and weight lifting. Pitchers also spend this time preparing for the next opponent.

A player's night does not end when the game is over, either. Many players use the time right after the game for

New York Mets third baseman David Wright talks with US Army veteran Helen Fumo during the 2013 All-Star weekend in New York.

weight lifting. This gives their bodies maximum time to recover for the next game. Players also have to speak with the press. Members of the press are briefly allowed into the clubhouse before that night's action. After each game the press comes back to ask questions about the game. When all is said and done, players might not get back home or to their hotel until after midnight.

The days are already long for MLB players. Constant travel makes them even longer. Teams are on the road for half the season. Sometimes these road trips last more than a week. And often teams travel at odd times. For example, a team might wrap up one game late at night and immediately head to the airport. These schedules require players to adapt to irregular sleep schedules.

"It's a lot of work," All-Star infielder Kevin Youkilis said of playing in the majors. "You come to the field and prepare yourself as best as you can. It's a really repetitive day,

Quotable

"I think that [being a role model] is something I take seriously. I remember some of my biggest role models growing up, besides my parents, were baseball players. So I understand that putting this jersey on every day, that I have an effect, whether I like it or not, on kids. And I try to act accordingly and provide at least some sort of positive view of a role model."
—David Wright, New York Mets All-Star third baseman

and there's a lot of flying across the country all the time. There's not much excitement. You don't get to do much [outside of work] during the year."

Still Having Fun

Players are together constantly from about February to October. Being a good teammate can be one of the most important keys to succeeding in the major leagues. Many players develop lifelong friendships.

In 2013, Los Angeles Dodgers infielder Juan Uribe formed a close friendship with pitcher Hyun-Jin Ryu. Uribe is from the Dominican Republic. His first language is Spanish, though he also speaks some English. Ryu, meanwhile, is from South Korea. He speaks Korean and knows very little English or Spanish. The root of their friendship is that both love to have fun. Becoming an All-Star requires hard work, but having fun goes a long way too.

"I like to get along with all of my teammates on every team that I have been on, and it's not any different here with the Dodgers and Ryu," said Uribe, a 13-year veteran. "In this game, you have to relax and have fun. You are not going to play better if you are nervous or too anxious. That's something I help Ryu with out there, and I think that's part of the reason I have had such a long career. I have fun in this game."

IN THE SPOTLIGHT

The long days and heavy travel schedules can be taxing on players. Boston Red Sox second baseman Dustin Pedroia has found a routine that helps him enjoy every day.

Pedroia, the 2008 AL MVP, arrives at the ballpark a good five hours before the game. He first goes through the essential duties. These include working out, putting his uniform on, taking batting practice, fielding ground balls, and stretching. Pedroia then makes a point to soak in the atmosphere. He will sit in the middle of the dugout and watch. He watches the grounds crew prepare the field. He watches fans make their way to their seats. He takes in the sounds and smells of a game that fill the stadium.

For Pedroia, few things are better than the transformation a ballpark goes through in the hours leading up to the game.

"That's what I'll remember when I retire—that feeling," he said.

CHAPTER FOUR

STAYING HEALTHY

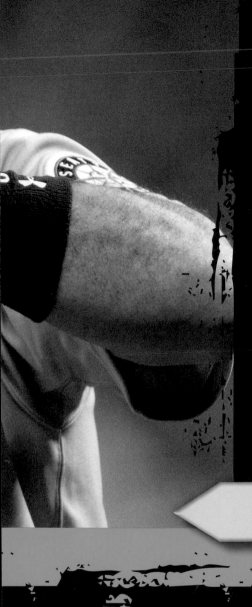

At 41 years old, Seattle Mariners outfielder Raul Ibanez was still going strong in 2013. It was his 18th season in the majors. And Ibanez smacked 29 home runs. That was just the third time in his career that he hit that many. The performance also tied a record. No player 41 or older had ever hit more home runs. Hall of Famer Ted Williams was also 41 when he hit 29 home runs in 1960.

"People ask me, 'Do you feel 41?' And I don't know what that's supposed to feel like," Ibanez said. "I don't really remember what it felt like to be 25, so it doesn't really matter. I feel good."

Seattle Mariners outfielder Raul Ibanez waits for a pitch during a 2013 game.

Younger ballplayers can sometimes get away with unhealthful habits. However, players such as Ibanez who thrive for many seasons must make health a priority. People's bodies break down as they get older. Those who have taken care of themselves and continue to do so hold up better as they age.

"Your training gets smarter and your eating habits get smarter and better," Ibanez said. "You learn how to do those things better."

Ibanez's long commitment to fitness proved to be valuable as he got older. Because he had a good base of fitness, he said he actually got stronger as he aged. In fact, Ibanez believed he was stronger at 41 than he had been five years earlier. However, he said he has to work more on areas such as foot speed and reflexes as he gets older.

Not Just for Veterans

Staying healthy certainly is not limited to the older players. Developing workout routines at a young age benefits players in

The DH

In 1973, the AL adopted the designated hitter (DH) rule. The rule allows for a player to bat in place of the pitcher. Pitchers then focus only on pitching. They are typically not great hitters anyway. So the rule results in a stronger bat in the lineup. The rule has also preserved the health and longevity of some great hitters. That is because the DH does not play in the field. Boston Red Sox slugger David Ortiz has benefited greatly from the rule. He was average as a first baseman. But Ortiz has been one of baseball's most feared hitters since becoming a regular DH in 2000. He was still a powerful hitter at the age of 37 in 2013. Ortiz hit 30 home runs that year.

several ways. Players who are in better shape perform better. Players who take care of their bodies when they are young also set themselves up to play longer.

Washington Nationals outfielder Bryce Harper started the 2013 season as a 20-year-old. Fans had high expectations for Harper. His fitness helped him reach those expectations. Harper hit 20 home runs for the second season in a row. He also made the All-Star Game for the second time in two years. Harper said he learned the importance of training from his father. Harper first began doing push-ups, sit-ups, and dips around the age of 13. That helped him develop a passion for training as he got older.

Players learn to adapt their workout plans throughout their careers. As Ibanez

Washington Nationals outfielder Bryce Harper sprints to third base during a 2013 game.

Los Angeles Dodgers outfielder Carl Crawford slides into home for the winning run against the San Francisco Giants in a 2013 game.

learned, the body changes with age. And for some players, they learn different training routines to help them get better.

Carl Crawford broke in with the Tampa Bay Devil Rays in 2002. He quickly became one of baseball's most exciting players. The outfielder led the AL in stolen bases four times from 2003–2007. However, he knew that his natural physical advantages would not last forever. Prior to the 2008 season, he put more of an emphasis on fitness. That emphasis included adding a gym to his home.

"Usually I just kind of sit around for two or three months [in the off-season]," he said. "This time I was able to keep my body tuned up nice and well until it was time to work out."

Diet and Nutrition

A good workout plan is just one key to long-term health. A good diet is just as important. Crawford learned that too. As a young player, he loved to eat fast food. However, he realized he could not continue eating it if he wanted to stay in great shape. And indeed, a more

Quotable

"There are a lot of things we do as athletes that fans don't get to see. The workouts, the off-season training. The amount of time we sacrifice away from our families to get in shape and to stay in shape."
—Baltimore Orioles first baseman Chris Davis. He led the majors with 53 home runs and 138 RBIs in 2013.

IN THE SPOTLIGHT

Texas Rangers first baseman Prince Fielder stands at 5 feet 11 inches (1.8 m) and weighs 275 pounds (125 kilograms). That makes him one of the heavier players in baseball. Still, physical fitness and proper nutrition have been important during his career. He is one of the best and most powerful hitters in the game. Fielder is also one of the most durable players. He became a regular in 2006. Through 2013, he had never missed more than five games in a season. Fielder said maintaining his health can be difficult, but he recognizes the importance of being in good physical condition.

"I have to, or else I'll get huge," he said. "Growing up, I was a big kid, so if I don't do something to at least stay from getting too big, I won't be able to play. So, that motivates me a lot because I want to be able to play, and not just play, but to be able to be durable and just be able to help the team, because if I'm overweight, I can't do anything."

healthful diet paid off. Crawford remains one of the best outfielders in baseball. After the 2011 season, he signed a new seven-year contract. That ensured he would be paid through the age of 35.

Proper nutrition also played a role in Ibanez still being a quality player at the age of 41. And in 2014, he signed a new one-year deal with the Los Angeles Angels. To stay healthy, he focuses on natural foods, such as fruits and vegetables. When he eats beef, he makes sure it is from grass-fed cattle. Grass-fed cattle are healthier and have more nutritious meat than cattle that are raised on feedlots. Also, in line with his healthful diet was a typical breakfast of three eggs, sweet potatoes, and kale.

Ibanez's diet and workout structure is unique to him, but many MLB players have similar plans. Paying close attention to physical health is an essential part of every player's success. The 162-game schedule of a major-league season can be brutal if players are not prepared and do not take care of themselves.

CHAPTER FIVE
STAYING SAFE

The pitcher's mound is just 60 feet 6 inches (18 m) from home plate. Pitchers end up several feet closer to home plate after delivery of a pitch. That means pitchers are in a dangerous position after every pitch.

J. A. Happ was on the mound for the Toronto Blue Jays on May 7, 2013. He delivered a pitch to Tampa Bay Rays batter Desmond Jennings. With a quick swing of the bat, Jennings smacked a line drive right back at Happ. The veteran pitcher had no time to react. The ball hit him squarely on the side of his head.

Toronto Blue Jays pitcher J. A. Happ lies on the ground after being hit in the head by a line drive in a 2013 game.

Emergency medical technicians (EMTs) quickly attended to Happ. The pitcher lay facedown on the mound for several minutes as they treated him. Finally, the EMTs stabilized Happ. They carted him off the field. Happ had suffered a fracture of his skull, just behind his left ear. Luckily for him, it was not a career-ending or life-threatening injury.

Happ returned to the mound three months later. However, the play was no fluke. During those three months, another pitcher took a ball off the head as well. The two plays showed why pitcher safety is one of the chief concerns among baseball officials.

"Guys are bigger now and hitting the ball harder and we're throwing the ball harder and when a guy hits one right on the screws bad things can happen," Cleveland Indians pitcher Vinnie Pestano said.

Equipment Improvements

In 1971, MLB started requiring that new players wear batting helmets.

Some position players have worn helmets in the field. Former All-Star John Olerud suffered

Quotable

"It's about safety. For me personally, when you have something on your head and it protects your life, it's important. Some people last year complained about it, saying it's a little bit heavy, a little bit weird, but I like it. . . . It's better for baseball."
—Milwaukee Brewers All-Star center fielder Carlos Gomez, talking about the new batting helmets that MLB players were required to wear starting in 2013. The helmet was designed to better protect the head.

a brain aneurysm while in college. A brain aneurysm is when a blood vessel balloons in the brain. A hard impact to Olerud's temple could have caused further damage. So he wore a batting helmet while manning first base for 17 seasons with five teams.

Justin Morneau was an MVP first baseman for the Minnesota Twins. In 2010, he slid into second base during a routine play. However, a fielder accidentally kneed Morneau's head. That resulted in a concussion for Morneau. It was more than a year before he was feeling right again. When Morneau came back, he wore a heavier, bulkier batting helmet.

Longtime MLB first baseman John Olerud wore a batting helmet while in the field as a precaution throughout his 17 major-league seasons.

Finding workable headgear for pitchers has proven more difficult. After Happ's injury, MLB medical director Dr. Gary Green said all the current options were either not

Justin Morneau struggled to regain his MVP form after suffering a concussion in 2010 while with the Minnesota Twins.

protective enough or too heavy. That finally changed after the 2013 season.

MLB introduced a padded cap for pitchers in January 2014. The new caps are designed with thick pads on the front and the sides. The pads offer extra protection to the upper head. But the caps are also nearly twice as heavy as normal caps. Players are not required to wear them.

Happ was optimistic about the new technology. However, he was initially unsure if he would wear the cap. "I'd have to see what the differences in feel would be—does it feel close enough to a regular cap?" he said. "You don't want to be out there thinking about it and have it take away from your focus on what you're doing."

Similar concerns were shared by other pitchers as well. The caps were considered just the first of many developments for this

Concussions

Concussions occur when somebody suffers a jolt to the head. The person loses some brain function. Usually the symptoms are temporary. Sometimes they can last for months or even forever. The Minnesota Twins know this well. In 2010, former MVP Justin Morneau suffered a concussion on a routine baserunning play. Morneau missed large parts of two seasons. He struggled to regain his form even after he returned. Twins catcher Joe Mauer is also a former MVP. In 2013, two balls slammed into Mauer's catcher's mask. They resulted in a concussion. Mauer ended up missing the final 39 games of the season. That off-season he decided to move permanently to first base. Another concussion could be career threatening. Mauer and the Twins determined he was less at risk playing first base.

issue. MLB said it would continue working to develop safer and less obstructive caps for pitchers.

Broken Bats

Some injuries are unavoidable. Other injuries can be limited or prevented, though. MLB is constantly looking into ways to improve player and fan safety. For example, the league started paying extra attention to bats.

In 2008, roughly one bat broke each game. That was the highest number in history. Players typically use bats made from one of two types of wood: ash or maple. Ash is a softer wood. Broken ash bats usually come apart cleanly. But many players prefer the stronger wood of maple bats. However, maple bats tend to break into sharp shards. These can be dangerous for fielders and fans. After the 2008 season, MLB worked with the US Forest Service to make bats safer. They found problems with how the bats were made. New rules were created to ensure bats were made better and broke cleaner. The changes helped the number of broken bats drop dramatically. In 2013, the rate of broken bats had been cut in half from the high in 2008.

"It is all about safety," MLB vice president for labor relations Dan Halem said. "That is the one reason we do all of this work."

IN THE SPOTLIGHT

It was 2011. San Francisco Giants catcher Buster Posey stood at home plate, awaiting the throw from the right fielder. Florida Marlins runner Scott Cousins raced toward home. Fans geared up for a collision. The ball got to Posey just before Cousins. But Cousins slammed into Posey, knocking the ball loose.

Cousins was safe. But Posey suffered a broken leg and three torn ankle ligaments. It was a huge blow to the Giants. Posey had been the NL Rookie of the Year in 2010.

Home plate collisions have been a part of the game for decades. However, injuries such as Posey's put collisions in the spotlight. Plays at the plate are some of the most exciting in baseball. But they are also very dangerous. Posey bounced back in 2012. He was the NL MVP and led the Giants to the World Series title. Following the 2013 season, MLB owners voted to ban home-plate collisions from the game.

CHAPTER SIX

PITCHING AND

Justin Verlander was at the top of his game. It was May 7, 2011. And for nine innings, the Detroit Tigers' pitcher dominated the Toronto Blue Jays. Verlander racked up just four strikeouts. But the All-Star right-hander allowed only one base runner, an eighth inning walk. The result was Verlander's second career no-hitter.

Verlander has been in control of most batters he has faced since 2006. He was the AL Rookie of the Year that year. In 2011, he accomplished a rare feat. Verlander won the AL Cy Young Award, given to the best pitcher in the league. He also was named the AL MVP. That award rarely goes to pitchers.

Detroit Tigers pitcher Justin Verlander throws the final pitch of a no-hitter against the Toronto Blue Jays on May 7, 2011.

CATCHING

The Tigers have become one of baseball's best teams since Verlander arrived. His presence showed the importance of an ace pitcher to a baseball team. MLB teams each have 25 active players. Five of those players are usually starting pitchers. Those pitchers usually pitch just once in every five games. But a great starter like Verlander can have a greater impact. The Tigers always have a good chance of winning when he is on the mound. That takes pressure off his teammates. And, his ability to often pitch late into games helps the bullpen. MLB teams usually carry seven or eight relief pitchers in the bullpen. The relievers pitch more often than starters but for fewer innings. Teams need to keep their best relief pitchers fresh. Having a workhorse starter such as Verlander is a good way to keep the relievers rested.

Quotable

"I want to play baseball. I think that's my job—to play baseball. I want to focus on what I love to do. . . . You can't do two things at the same time. When you do that, lonel is going to be wrong. I don't want to be wrong on what I have to do—my real job."
—Detroit Tigers infielder Miguel Cabrera on why he does not do many endorsements and instead focuses on the game

A Demanding Job

Pitching looks easy. Pitching in the majors, however, is very

Los Angeles Dodgers pitcher Clayton Kershaw pitches against the New York Yankees in 2013. Kershaw won the NL Cy Young Award that year.

technical. Pitchers put spin on their pitches. Spin makes the ball move while in flight. Pitchers such as Verlander spend years developing these pitches.

Performance-Enhancing Drugs (PEDs)

Baseball players during the late 1990s and the early 2000s appeared stronger than ever. There was a reason for that. It was later determined that many players of that era used PEDs. The most noticeable impact was on baseball's home run records. The single-season home run record of 61 had stood since 1961. Between 1998 and 2001, players surpassed 61 six times. All the players who hit more than 61 homers were later linked to PEDs. Using PEDs is cheating. PEDs are also dangerous to one's health. MLB finally began cracking down on PED use in the 2000s. The league put new procedures in place to test players and punish those found using.

A lot goes into great pitching besides throwing the ball. Pitchers need to perfect every movement of their bodies when they throw. Hitters study pitchers. The hitters will notice if a pitcher's delivery differs from one type of pitch to another. If the pitcher's delivery does differ, hitters can figure out which pitch is coming. In addition, pitchers must have strong arms and legs. Flexibility and balance bring everything together.

Pitching can be taxing on the body. Starting pitchers often throw approximately 100 pitches per game. Each game is a strenuous test of the muscles in the pitching arm, the legs, and the core muscles. How pitchers hold up as the game goes on can make or break the start. Verlander said that staying strong is a

mix between
physical fitness
and recovery time.

"My endurance
as a pitcher and
recovery [from each
start] is the main
thing," Verlander said.
"During the season,
recovery is probably
the biggest thing for
me, to be able to get
ready for that next
start. Having your
body in good shape
allows you to do
that."

San Francisco Giants catcher Buster Posey, *left*, talks with pitcher Tim Lincecum during a 2012 game.

Behind the Plate

Pitchers start each play in baseball by throwing the ball to home plate. Catchers play a major role in each play too. The best catchers do much more than just receive pitches. They also work with pitchers to manage the game. Catchers study each opponent. They learn which pitches will get each batter out. Then they work with the pitcher to execute their game plan. As such, behind a great pitching performance is often a great catching performance.

Teams often look for catchers who work well with pitchers, even if the catcher is just an average hitter.

IN THE SPOTLIGHT

Yadier Molina is part of a generation of catchers who thrive in all aspects of baseball. The St. Louis Cardinals' catcher is known for his defense, his game management, and his hitting.

When Molina first took up catching, he spent countless hours working on fundamentals. Early on, fans most appreciated Molina's defense. He was an expert at throwing out base runners and blocking balls. From 2008 to 2013, he won a Gold Glove Award every season. Over the years, Molina developed into a great hitter as well. From 2011 to 2013, he had a .313 batting average and averaged 74 RBIs and 35 doubles per season. What pitchers notice most, however, is his game management.

"He does a great job of studying hitters along with us, knowing our pitchers, our strengths," former Cardinals pitcher Kyle Lohse said.

Jason Varitek had a .256 career batting average. Yet he was a key player for the Boston Red Sox for 14 seasons. Boston won the 2004 and 2007 World Series with Varitek behind the plate.

Teammates noted Varitek's ability to work well with pitchers. He spent hours outside of games studying opposing hitters. And he knew the strengths and weaknesses of his own pitchers. During games, he often knew the best pitches to throw to get a batter out. Pitcher Matt Clement signed with the Red Sox before the 2005 season. He said that playing with Varitek influenced his decision.

Catching can take a huge toll on one's body, however. Catchers have to squat for each pitch. That puts pressure on their knees, ankles, and backs. And catchers have to use their entire bodies to block pitches. These challenges result in catchers generally needing more rest than other everyday players.

Pitchers and catchers are important to any baseball team. But a World Series contender needs a deep roster. Nine players start each game. Position players must be able to get hits, move runners, drive in runs, and play fundamental defense. Teams also need bench players who can come in and provide support as base runners, pinch hitters, or defensive replacements. When all of these players come together, they can create a season to remember.

Train Like a Pro

Longtime MLB second baseman Brandon Phillips is a great hitter and a great fielder. In 2013, Phillips won an NL Gold Glove Award for the fourth time in his career. His work begins early in January.

Phillips does several exercises to improve his defense.

1. Phillips often starts his workouts with what he calls "wall ball." This entails throwing a ball against a wall and trying to catch it in the middle of his body. It helps loosen up his hands.

2. Next, he works on catching the ball from the side so he can work on his backhand catches.

3. Phillips will also do a lot of work with his bare hands. He will have someone roll him the ball, and he will catch it with his glove hand and then his throwing hand. This allows him to get comfortable with the feeling of the ball in his hands.

4. Next up is a side-to-side drill. With someone rolling the ball to him, Phillips shuffles his feet from side to side to get into position to catch the ball in the middle of his body. This helps to prepare for ground balls that take bad hops.

5. In another exercise, Phillips gets on his knees and has someone hit the ball to him so he can work on catching the ball in front of him. Phillips said he does this because it works the hands and it helps make catching the ball easier when he stands up.

Baseball Equipment Diagram

Bat
All bats in MLB are made of wood, but each player selects the size and weight of his bat.

Batting Helmet
When batting and running the bases, players must wear a helmet for protection.

Batting Gloves
Most hitters wear gloves to help grip the bat. Gloves also limit the shock to the hands when the bat hits the ball.

Pads
Some hitters wear extra pads on their elbows or shins for added protection from pitches or foul balls.

Uniform
Baseball players on each team must wear matching jerseys, pants, and hats. Some players pull their pants up to show their socks.

Shoes
Baseball players wear cleats to get better traction in the field.

Glossary

ace: the best starting pitcher on a team

amateur: unpaid. High school and college athletes must compete as amateurs.

assist: when a fielder throws out a base runner

contract: an agreement between a team and a player that determines years of service, salary, and other working arrangements

draft: a system by which teams in a league select incoming talent

endurance: the ability to perform for an extended period

fielding percentage: a statistic that shows a player's effectiveness on the field by comparing a player's total putouts and assists over the player's total putouts, assists, and errors

injury: a physical problem that often prevents a player from competing

no-hitter: a game in which the opposing team does not reach base through a hit

off-season: the time of year when a league is inactive

prospect: a player with potential to compete in the major leagues

putout: a play that retires a batter or base runner

rookie: a first-year player

scout: a person who seeks out talent for a professional team

veteran: a player who has lots of experience

For More Information

Baseball America
http://www.baseballamerica.com
This site is a one-stop shop for information about up-and-coming baseball players.

Baseball Prospectus
http://www.baseballprospectus.com
There is no shortage of baseball news and analysis on this site.

Editors of *Sports Illustrated*. *Sports Illustrated Baseball's Greatest*. New York: Time Home Entertainment, 2013.
This book offers the top 10 in a variety of baseball categories, including best ballpark and the best player ever at each position.

Kennedy, Mike, and Mark Stewart. *Long Ball: The Legend and Lore of the Home Run*. Minneapolis: Millbrook Press, 2006.
Read all about some of the most exciting home runs in baseball history in this book packed full of photos and statistics.

MLB Player Workouts
http://www.mlbplayerworkouts.com
This site is filled with different workouts done by MLB players.

National Baseball Hall of Fame. *Inside the Baseball Hall of Fame: The National Baseball Hall of Fame and Museum*. New York: Simon & Schuster, 2013.
Get a behind-the-scenes look at the Baseball Hall of Fame and Museum in Cooperstown, New York, with this book.

Stack—Baseball Workouts
http://www.stack.com/baseball
Check out this site for videos and other information about the workouts MLB players do to stay in shape.

Turbow, Jason. *The Baseball Codes: Beanballs, Sign Stealing, and Bench-Clearing Brawls: The Unwritten Rules of America's Pastime*. New York: Pantheon Books, 2010.
There is more to baseball than meets the eye. This book offers a look at some of the unwritten rules and quirky traditions from baseball history.

Source Notes

6   "Derek Jeter and His Hard Work Heritage—Jordan Interview 2009," YouTube video, 2:02, posted by "cooler316619," July 4, 2009, http://www.youtube.com/watch?v=hLNuA1xw31c.

11 "Troy Tulowitzki on His Fielding Technique," *Stack*, June 8, 2012, http://www.stack.com/video/1505170892001/Troy-Tulowitzki-on -His-Fielding-Technique/.

18 "Evan Longoria's Hitting Drills," *Stack*, May 20, 2010, http://www .stack.com/video/86911564001/Evan-Longorias-Hitting-Drills/.

20 Mike Gegenheimer, "Former Zephyr Ed Lucas Finally Gets His Shot with the Miami Marlins at Age 31," *New Orleans Times-Picayune*, June 21, 2013, http://www.nola.com/zephyrs/index. ssf/2013/06/31-year -old_former_zephyr_fina.html.

21 Derek Jeter, with Jack Curry, *The Life You Imagine* (New York: Three Rivers Press, 2000), 37.

23 Lou Schuler, "Bryce Harper: The Fast Learner," *Men's Health*, March 25, 2013, http://www.menshealth.com/fitness/bryce -harper.

25 Ibid.

31 Meggie Zahneis, "Wright Embraces Being Looked Up to as Role Model," *MLB.com*, August 6, 2012, http://mlb.mlb.com/news /article.jsp?ymd=20120806&content_id=36210728&vkey =breakingbarriers.

31–32 Kevin Youkilis, personal interview with author, June 23, 2010.

32 Jesse Sanchez, "Odd Couple: Ryu, Uribe Become Best of Friends," *MLB.com*, October 6, 2013, http://mlb.mlb.com/news/article/mlb /odd-couple-hyun-jin-ryu-juan-uribe-become-best-of-friends?ymd =20131006&content_id=62565708&vkey=news_mlb.

33 Peter Abraham, "The Art of Being Dustin Pedroia," *Boston Globe*, July 14, 2013, http://www.bostonglobe.com/sports/2013/07/13 /dustin-pedroia-and-love-game/Q3v8ExJQp35ugZVVPfUmFM /story.html.

35 Jim Caple, "Ibanez's Fountain (and Kale) of Youth," *ESPN*, July 10, 2013, http://espn.go.com/mlb/story/_/id/9463503/raul-ibanez -secrets-successful-mlb-life-40.

36 Ibid.

39 Bill Chastain, "Diet, Exercise Paying Off for Crawford," *MLB.com*, March 2, 2008, http://mlb.mlb.com/news/article.jsp?ymd =20080301&content_id=2399645&vkey=spt2008news&fext =.jsp&c_id=tb.

39 Steve Melewski, "With MLB Suspensions Coming, Chris Davis Talked about PEDs over the Weekend," *MASNHD*, August 5, 2013, http://www.masnsports.com/steve_melewski/2013/08 /with-mlb-suspensions-coming-chris-davis-talked-about-peds-over -the-weekend.html.

40 "Prince on His Workout Routines," *MLB.com*, June 20, 2011, http://wapc.mlb.com/play/?content_id=16093135.

44 Rick Freeman, Associated Press, "Pitcher Safety against Liners Still Issue for MLB," *Yahoo News*, June 19, 2013, http://news .yahoo.com/pitcher-safety-against-liners-still-issue-mlb -074446337.html.

44 Mark Newman, "MLB Begins League-Wide Use of Rawlings Helmet," *MLB.com*, February 20, 2013, http://losangeles .dodgers.mlb.com/news/article.jsp?ymd=20130220&content _id=41824300&vkey=news_mlb&c_id=mlb.

47 ESPN.com news services, "J.A. Happ Suffered Skull Fracture," *ESPN*, August 29, 2013, http://espn.go.com/mlb/story/_/id /9252253/ja-happ-toronto-blue-jays-skull-fracture-placed-15-day -disabled-list.

47 William Weinbaum, "Pitchers' Protective Caps Approved," *ESPNLA*, January 28, 2014, http://espn.go.com/los-angeles /story/_/id/10363291/pitchers-protective-caps-approved-major -league-baseball.

48 Quinn Roberts, "Huge Strides Being Made in Reducing Broken Bats," *MLB.com*, August 3, 2012, http://mlb.mlb.com/news /article.jsp?ymd=20120803&content_id=36046676.

52 Jon Paul Morosi, "Cabrera's Fame Lagging behind His Bat," *Fox Sports*, June 6, 2013, http://msn.foxsports.com/mlb/story /miguel-cabrera-best-hitter-in-baseball-game-like-lebron-james -popularity-far-behind-gets-lost-in-a-crowd-060513.

55 "Pitching Drills with Justin Verlander," *Stack*, June 26, 2008, http://www.stack.com/video/1631227745/pitching-drills-with -justin-verlander/.

56 Jeff Gordon, "Cards Game Day with Jeff Gordon," *St. Louis Post-Dispatch*, October 9, 2012, http://live.stltoday.com/Event /Cards_Game_Day_with_Jeff_Gordon_4?Page=0.

Index

About the Author

Brian Howell is a freelance writer based in Denver, Colorado. He has been a sports journalist for 20 years, writing about high school, college, and professional athletics. In addition, he has written books about sports and history. A native of Colorado, he lives with his wife and four children in his home state.

Photo Acknowledgments

The images in this book are used with the permission of: © Mark Goldman/Icon SMI, pp. 3 (top), 12–13, 22–23, 46; © Brad Rempel/Icon SMI, pp. 3 (middle), 16–17; © Zuma Press/Icon SMI, pp. 3 (bottom), 40, 50–51, 56; © Anthony J. Causi/Icon SMI, pp. 4–5, 6–7; © Library of Congress, p. 8 LC-DIG-bbc-0411f; © Daniel Gluskoter/Icon SMI, p. 11; © Rich Barnes/Icon SMI, p. 14; © Cliff Welch/Icon SMI, pp. 19, 24, 42–43; © Juan Salas/Icon SMI, p. 20; © Frank Orris/Icon SMI, pp. 26–27; © Scott Kane/Icon SMI, p. 28; © Rich Graessle/Icon SMI, pp. 30–31; © Icon SMI, p. 33; © Juan DeLeon/Icon SMI, pp. 34–35; © Jeff Moffett/Icon SMI, p. 37; © Wally Caddow/Icon SMI, pp. 38–39; © Douglas Jones/Icon SMI, p. 45; © Kelley L Cox/Icon SMI, p. 49; © Chris Williams/Icon SMI, pp. 52–53; © Tony Medina/Icon SMI, p. 55; © John Cordes/Icon SMI, p. 59.

Front cover: © Jim Davis/The Boston Globe via Getty Images, (main); © Valentina Razumova/Shutterstock.com (stadium lights).

Main body text set in Eurostile LT Pro 12/18. Typeface provided by Linotype.